The Wild Awake

The Wild Awake

*A Reading from the
Erotic Compass of the World*

Paulann Petersen

CONFLUENCE PRESS

A JAMES R. HEPWORTH BOOK

I am grateful to John Daniel, W.S. DiPiero, Kenneth Fields, and the late Denise Levertov—all of the writing program at Stanford—for their faith in my early work. To Diane Averill, Jim Grabill, Verlena Orr, Greg Simon, and Sandra Williams, I give thanks for insightful readings of many of these poems in their initial drafts.
—Paulann Petersen

Publication of Confluence Press books is made possible, in part, by the generosity of Lewis-Clark State College, Washington State University and The Idaho Commission on the Arts.

Cover illustration by Josie Gray.
Dustjacket, cover and interior design by Robin L. Watkins.
Paulann Petersen's photo by Greg Wahl-Stephens.

ISBN: 1-881090-43-4 (P)
ISBN: 1-881090-44-2 (C)
Library of Congress Control Number: 2001099909
First Edition 10 9 8 7 6 5 4 3 2 1

Published by:
Confluence Press, Inc.
Lewis-Clark State College
500 Eighth Avenue
Lewiston, ID 83501
(208) 799-2336

Distributed by:
Midpoint Trade Books
1263 Southwest Boulevard
Kansas City, KS 66103
(913) 831-2233
Fax (913) 362-7401

For Ken, who is this book's haven.

&

For Greg, who gave it shape.

Contents

A Reading from the
Erotic Compass of the World

❦

A Reading from the Erotic Compass of the World

Pleasure's arrow, you've swung
in the direction of the one heaven.
Pleasure's dart, you align
with marrow of the world.

Little tongue of wild greed,
you waggle toward the stars,
the swollen moon. You shiver to seek
their hunger-sprung light.

Let yourself wobble and ache.
Dip, kowtow your tip,
point at that deep, deepest well,
its rim: thick rime of salt.

You are a brassy bud,
honey's one sharp drop—
jitter of pollen getting a fix on
your own homemade sun.

Not an Angel

Wings of my desire grow—
I swear, they do—
from my breastbone
under my very eyes,
from this uneasy place
easing out, easing in
with each dizzy swell of breath.

Unholy at best, they sprout,
spreading feather by feather,
each plume escaping
its gaudy sisters
like fingers of an opening fan.

Enough to have such wings
and not be an angel.
But here! between
my breasts—their wild rustle
coaxing my nipples into
fierce knots of unrest.

Why can't these wings
sprout from my shoulders?
Then if I turned
my back away, I could be
a little discreet.

But no. Lifting away
to pump in front of my body,
they wag me around as if
I were a wisp of smoke.

Of course I wear oversized coats.
Of course I keep my arms
folded across my chest.
I'm afraid their huge
flapping will churn
the air in this room,

will set forth
an irreparable storm—
first here and there
and over there—of sighs,
of heartbeat racket
wherever I go.

Timepiece

Desire, that feathered clock—
      quill-quick downy-slow—
beats time with its wings,
    glides toward me without a
      whisper of ruffled air.

Oh, and when desire goes
    walking! stiff-legged
      click click   winding up
      tight   winding down
I feel each step   each
      prickly stab of heat.

Cloth

Some clothes I wear for their excess.
Body stretched long, I lie
on my side so the plenty
of a certain dress can fall away
from my breasts and stomach
and thighs like a river,
slow and easy in the eddy.

This is a fine way to lie
on a bit of lawn and wait for the man
who says he would be my lover,
wait and wonder at how our bodies
could fit, in their strangeness,
one to the other—how strangers,
untaught, could ever become lovers.

Stretched long on the grass,
my right side attempts to match
the given flat of the ground, hard,
a line that throws my left side
akimbo—jut and jump
of shoulder and hipbone,
jagged motion into the air.

Soft cloth falls away
from my skin in the way

a grace streams from bodies together.
Tender, that remarkable flow
from two headlong bodies
thrown askew in their rush to fit,
to press themselves into each other.

Promise

I want this man to slip his hand
under my hair, then take
my nape in his hold—boldly,
without hesitation—so the hair
is a dark curtain surrounding this
place where our bodies first touch.

I will grow my hair in a heavy
fall down my back; along that skin
his hand might touch, I will spend,
drop by drop, what I have of perfume—
musk, magnolia, heat. I will,
for this. For a chance of this.

From Afar

Oh quick-step   break-neck
rambler   loose limb
move in
a little closer
fire my face with my own chagrin
start my throat pumping
with the rat-a-tat
of your flicker-fan hands

one step out
one step in
shim shim shimmer skin
give me another little sip
of your fine
honeysuckle
sweet from the flower-mouth
wine

Merman

Mother told me there'd be
all kinds—

he-men, beefcakes, pretty-boys,
wolves—but she never

mentioned *this:* someone
who'd risk it all just to rock

in the caulky cradle of a boat;
a man who says he could

walk into a mountain lake
keep walking, and breathe;

a lover who craves
the taste of salt inside me.

Oriental Lilies

Theirs is not the smell
of sex. No. Theirs is more
a sweetness, liquid and heady.
Morels smell of sex—
that first sharp scratch of salt
then the dank earth opening up.
A certain fruit in the market
smells like sex. The one with an
unpronounceable name.
A small sign says *cut me in half,*
eat my pulp with a spoon.
Lifting its brown globe
to my face and breathing
in, I'm shocked—
as when in a dream I find
I'm naked. The air a cool
insistence on my skin. Lilies.
A room and a half away,
I smell them—petals
marked with thick, burgundy drops,
each anther a dangling worm
of red powder, anthem of pollen.
I move to where they rest
on a low table, twisting my head
to look into a blossom, pale cave
of perfume.
        Too close.

Nose, fingertip, cheek,
fingers, palm, sleeve of my blouse,
collar, throat   now smeared
with red, with saffron—
swift, disarming stain.

Graveyard Narcissus

Its two-part bulb,
like a double chamber,
swells from under a rib's cage.

Succulent roots feed in the depth
of rust that was blood.
Each bloom is a broad

moon, with a sun
caught small in its crux—
the sun at last

revealed for what it is,
fountain of pollen
surrounded by the light it lends.

Even so, what I crave
is this flower's perfume,
each breath a spun honey

dissolving my lungs.
Some pining heart's
signal from the grave—

its dumb light
a silence from its own
white and yellow sorrow—

is hardly perfume.
I need what I can breathe,
and with each breath

smell. Not the heart's show,
but that one story
only the heart can tell.

Small Acts of Devotion

A flower has vines green and blue
to weave a blue-green shadow,
backdrop to the moist blossom's
extravagant call for attention.

Deep leaf hollow, twining niche,
that temple of the flower
is not unlike the thin-skinned spot
to one side of an eye:

temple of a loved one,
destination for my eyes
when, our long gaze broken,
he takes a sidelong glance.

His temple marbled with veins
is destination for my lips, having faith
I could weight his eyelids, stir
what pulses there with my kiss.

Or if not with the touch of my lips,
surely then with my tongue's tip—
my mouth against his veined skin
a damp flower open again.

Mirror of These Eyes

Turn the quicksilvered glass
against a wall. Shut the oval
of burnished brass deep in a drawer.
Turn your back to picture windows,
to pools of water, smooth and clear.
Make your mirror from my eyes.

What can reflection tell you
but lies? How could light
bent away from what it seeks
give anything back but doubt
and sighs? Make of my eyes your
only mirror, mirror in these eyes.

Let these portals to my heart
show you truth much deeper
than any glass could recognize.
Look at me and see what I see
while looking at you: myself
loved in a lover's eyes.

A Bride of the World

The world is my lover,
I shall not want.

It curves its hands
around my ribs, and my bones
comply: twins
to its pliant fingers.
I carry the echo
of its circling shapes—
this cradle, inside.

It dips my body into the pigment
of light, leaves my print
wherever I lie—
smudge of nipple and belly,
stipple of my inmost thigh.
In its bottomless water,
the surging of my body subsides.

It feeds my tongue
with honey, with sea,
with an oil, pungent and warm,
pressed from fields of seed.
My mouth is the cup
of its offering. The table I set
white as a wing.

In a valley steeped with shadow
and dusk, with clotting dark,
my breath catches. Again
my breathing startles and veers
like a swallow's retort
in flight. I fear, am soothed.
I blaze, I quake.

Surely this trembling will stay
with my flesh until
my ending day. Surely my body
is given away, carried over
the threshold—lifted
by a lover's embrace
into the house of this world.

Speaking of Dreams

Out from the dark bramble,
you find yourself.
Again *you,* you move into
daylight, awake beneath grayed
sky still filled with sleep.

Whatever passageways you crawled,
whatever tunnels within
that warren of berry briars:
all *whatevers* close behind you
seamless as the green, watery

tangle they were, they are.
A scratch rising
in a string of tiny beads
heals as swiftly as your glance
vainly trying to find it

on your arm. What you ate
back there—how sweet, how tart,
how many and bitter, how gleamed
with the dark of old blood—
you do not know.

Purple that shadows your fingertips
is new, maybe not, maybe so,
but odd. *Strange:* only the stain

on your tongue—the one
you'll be the last

to see, stain thick with
thorn and ferment,
with blooms swallowed whole
by swollen night—only it gives
your former whereabouts away.

Feral

I bleed in a dream.
My hand, clamped
around the muzzle of threat,
lets go. Those milky
teeth are free,
and I bleed

with no reason
for fear. It's just
color, really
and the lightheaded
reel at the sight
of that color: rush of

wild poppies. Two, three,
a whole rash field,
strew of wet silk
then a fine dust
floating from one black
throat to another.

I let blood in a dream.
No loss, no loss—
it's merely a step toward
waking, a trail of scent
I leave for each
dream animal to follow.

In Dreams

—after Wislawa Szymborska

In the midst of weather
a mountain makes for
only itself,
I find myself.

Clear as day
I see what I didn't
at the time.

Leaving my torn skin,
blood carries
no pain in its red.

My beating arms at last
take hold in air;
each high note is just
below my reach.

A man whose anger
once paralyzed me
has one blue,
one yellow eye.

The dead,
quite simply,
are not.

Utterly foreign,
some language leaves
a word for waking breath.

That key
I'm so frantic to find
opens nothing,
after all.

What You Didn't Know About Money

It's the bride who wears
a yellow shoe, the butcher shop
that's always closed,
elective surgery, either/or,
the lake you thought
you'd never fish.
Dos-si-dos and serial sex

are it, and the one word
that rhymes with every other.
Empty quiver, Mother-
may-I, easily a better door
than any window. Money's
the last thing you dreamed
you'd ever do.

The Day I Became a Woman

The night before, I dreamed
of a tree outside the door
pruned so severely just
blunt limbs remained.
From its trunk at ground level,
out of the damp soil,
huge red leaves fanned—
incredibly bigger and brighter
than the few russet scraps
scattered around.

Early that morning I found
a hummingbird dead on the step,
so drab I first saw
a withered flower—
but when I picked it up
the throat feathers changed
from brown to a red
beyond belief. I stood
for a time, turning my hand
so the red caught
and faded, caught and faded.
The hummingbird's beak was
closed so tightly
it seemed of one piece,
like the finest, dark thorn
I'd ever see.

Then She Is the Garden

Under the needle, her skin jerks
in lightning spasms she can't will away.
She stares hard at the tattooer's chart—
dragons, eagles, coiled snakes.
He urges her to try a heart, a dove
while she still has room, but knows
she'll take only flowers and vines.

The last time she let a man have his way,
he set two lamps by the unmade bed
and would not take his eyes from her skin.
She closed hers, red seeping inside the lids.
He entered her as if he parted
the stems of some fragile bouquet.

She dreams of babies.
In these dreams she can't see
herself. It's cold there, and only
what lives on her skin
can thrive in such ice.
A baby reaches toward her,
teeth spaced apart in pink gums,
skin so tender she can see
a branch of veins on one temple.
Its breath enters the air
like the pale uncurling of a fern.

Nights when her skin seems to swell,
and even the lightest cloth is too much,
she walks her darkened room,
unaware of mirrors.
Then there's no mistake. She is
the naked garden, orchid of ink,
tendril of painted blood.

Second Skin

Even on days when the sun clears
everything out of the sky, when ditchweeds
and fences and the stairstep of shrubs
are flattened by its insistence, even then
you can choose the moon.

Snubbing the sun, you can turn yourself
to that pale smudge just visible
in the simmer of blue above.
Call it drop of thin milk
or the ghost's half eye—

whatever name, you can take the day
to follow its course in an overheated sky,
brooding on secondhand light,
blood sisters,
salty kisses and lies.

At night things cool down.
Another moon shines unfocused
from behind a scrim of clouds, reminder
that while you were choosing your
daylight moon, the sun

didn't wait to one side.
Somehow the sun left its mark on you.
But that's not news.

You've carried it with you before
in darkness, in daylight, for days.

Little engine of borrowed heat,
apple of one fierce eye,
face it: you're back to that
oldest thing under the sun.
Call yourself ocean-shifter,

the dream's one beacon, say you're
a bowl in the sky full
to the brink and gleaming until
you're ready to change again,
until you shed another skin.

To Dream a Lover Away

Let your dream carry him
away, and by that very
dreaming, put him
at arm's length where you may
examine at leisure
his exact shadowy shape,
maybe even come to terms
with his voice, its narcotic
ways and by-the-ways.

How dream you, Sweetness?
you might ask of him
as you dream right past
his swift, disarming glance,
moving on to explore
those ample lips,
his oh so heavy eyelids
half lowered—seeing all this
with your decidedly
undreamy, dreaming eyes.

Take him all in. Take his own
sweet time. Keep in mind
this dreaming lets you
linger on what's bound to be
too close, too wide
for the focus of your

open eyes. So linger along.
Have your way with him,
your own easy-does-it take
on what's waiting in
the wild awake.

Perfume

Perfume

A woman who carries the scent
of sleep. A dream where a lover
appears as words he's whispered
against her neck, then as
silent gesture. That pressure
of his hand along her thigh—
wild current to seize her awake.

She smells of the laundry
she pinned to a clothesline
as a girl, her skin still keeping
soap and sun driven into its weave
by wind, her lips pursed
as if they held clothespins
to free her gesturing hands.

Her hands are branches of trees
that sough in deep forest,
the stillness robbing such trees
of speech. They are dusty sparrows
skimming back and forth.
Her own hands are a scent moving
into then out of her reach.

Snow Red

She's the beauty sleeping in that
other fairy tale, the story
too adult for kids.

In it, the briar hedge
around her father's castle
doesn't keep much out.
Those men who come and go at will
have their way with her.

After her body swells to bursting,
someone puts the baby's
mouth to her breast. For her,
that fierce tug might as well be
part of a dream.

Waking at last she feels her skin
prickle with what it recalls,
ready to spill the story.
But what does she know
of recounting such things?

She skims her hands
down her body. *Untouched*: of that
she's certain, although she can taste
some piece of another world
still caught in her throat.

Staring at herself in a mirror's
blank gaze, she sees
only beauty. And begins to age.

A Natural History

These days the trees grow
flushed with their own fever.
They set forth a froth of pink
on their branches—

countless flecks up and down
dark limbs, columns of heat
wavering into the sky. I could say
this color is like a ribbon

of tender agate,
or that gloss within a shell
from the sea. No.
It's clearly blood

suffusing their even flesh
canted wide to the wind and sun,
blood keeping a
rash promise to spring.

These are the trees surrounding
the room where I sleep.
Returning at night, I find
the scent of blossom makes

a path to my bed. I see air
carry off bits of the trees' fever

then deliver them to the ground.
With each footstep I stir

what's fallen,
what darkness has turned
to a cool startle of white—
that indelible color of loss.

Room

Summer is that room where I
can be naked, am naked,
touched and touching,

my tongue and my lover's tongue
so much the same I hardly know
how to speak. I speak a lie.

There is no lover, only
this hurt. Only my nakedness,
my need to be within this room.

Here, the wings of a swallow
heat up the air with work
so my body can learn the working

of bodies. Here, the moon
presses her crescent of milk
on a sun-struck sky

so the words from sleep can linger.
Somewhere in summer's room
a pine marten waits

for a fisherman to toss aside
the rosy entrails of a trout—
while the one gold spot

on the marten's dark fur
burns at her throat.
Something swells in my throat,

is gone, then swells again.
Here is the chance for learning
and unlearning. The bruise

rises, takes hard shape,
finds its depth and boundary.
Body stretched, arms lifted,

I reach above me, but fail to find
an end to summer. No roof,
no ceiling, no cloud-held sky.

Every peril, sweet and heavy
in the heat of falling,
plummets toward me, inside.

Lullaby

Now the hour is black, the moments
invisible. I have kept the night
awake with hunger. Want and must
jostle within me, turning my body
from side to side to side.

Whirling beyond my sight
are the stars. Beyond my heartbeat
a single voice rings. Like a gull
on an updraft, its effortless note,
this word that floats—*sleep*.

Night is a darkness only to eyes
that lie open. *Sleep sleep.*
Clothed in silk of borrowed light,
a moon already rises
on dream's jagged horizon.

A Little Primer on Sleep

Inside the sleep of a magpie
who speaks in tongues of oil,
is milk, asleep, black and depthless.
In the sleep of honey repeated
from chamber to chamber,
lies a struck match.

A crossword puzzle sleeps itself fulfilled,
letters snug in their cloisters.
The moon shaves off bits of darkness
with each shallow breath.
Sleeping mirrors
see themselves as ever awake.

Locked in the sleep of blood,
in its exact stillness,
is salt's sleep, a tide turning.
Inside the sleep of a white paper sack—
most of its length twisted shut
to hold the orange within—
a comet has come to rest.

Haven

Come, Love, and rest
your sleep in me.
Let our two sleeps
slip back and forth between

our selves in a tide
rising—our breath
the night's deep wave.
I will hurt nothing in you

as you eddy and surge,
as we swell, drift,
first into, then out of our
one body.

Only by the faint taste
of morning's salt on our skin
will we know how far
we have been.

Calling

What habits of love
do you teach me? What habits
will I someday have to break?
I stay awake until the moon
appears and disappears,
waiting for your call.
I fall asleep before the sun
eases its light out of the sky,
hoping my sleep will be pierced
by the sound of your voice,
sweet and dusky—skirting my body,
drifting inside my skin
like a coarse, narcotic smoke.

Some say the air contains
atoms breathed by the Buddha.
How could it not hold some part
of what you breathe into your body,
then breathe out again?
Once we stood close enough
to exchange breaths, back and forth.
Our hands, the length of our
clothed bodies touched.
How can I now breathe in
and not breathe you?

What do your lips taste like
right now? Are they sweet?
Salty? Oh, I know.
Both. When I finally kiss you,
tracing the outline
of your lips with my tongue,
that taste will be salt and straw,
honey and smoke.

The moon outside is full.
The moon inside is almost
full. From its one ragged edge
a pale milk flows across the sheet,
the pillow, across the taut
desire weighing my limbs.

What hour chimes from the clock
in the room where you sleep?
Here, longing tells its own time,
with a dream's slowness
of motion, with my heart's
swift, uneven beat.

Where the Animal Goes
When I Am Awake

After my last breath of sleep
breaks against the oncoming day,
he leaves my body and rises
with me—my upright shadow,
there: wherever I go.
After he eases the heavy curve
of dream from my limbs,
after the smoke of his skin
has drifted from my blood,
my skin, mine is the black
to his white. Where I am
light, he is darkness.

       I taste the bitter, and he
is the effortless river's reflection.
Where my tongue touches salt,
his is the sigh at the base of my throat.
To my scatter and snip, he is breathe and skim,
he is with me. When I hedge each step,
he sallies, he's there.
After the day lies picked apart
by sunlight, after the night lies
staring ahead, mute as a god, he
turns to me, turns into me. I return.

For the Love of Sleep

Sleep, your pet, erotic toy,
curls its limbs around
your limbs, silkens
its fur and skin against
your easing breath,
then rolls onto its back.

Here you sink, you drift beside
its feral heat. Each rise
and fall of your chest is
caress. Each clasp, unclasp
of your heart is a stroke
lingered along the down
of that underbelly—
flushed with dream—
abandoned only to you.

Words Rise
From Nowhere Else

&

Words Rise
From Nowhere Else

Despite the whisper of death,
each day my heart pumps out
its strange and lovely litany,
marks out a notation of lurching blood
whether I take note of its rhythm
or not. I can make my lungs stop—
for a while—their swell and collapse,
hold them still for a blue
and dizzying count, but cannot hold
my heart from its stroking.
What if, to keep its beat,
I had to remember how my heart
is a heart, had to recall the way
of its work each second second?
I would be speechless.
Surely this poem that is
my life would stop.

Fabrication

Tell a lie about a cloud-filled
sky at night, a lie
about the moon it hides.
Tell another about the first scattered
drops of rain from those clouds

baffling only-heaven-can-know
which of the moon's phases. Say there's
a woman looking out a window
into the night muffled by that moon-taker,
thickened and now falling.

Tell what the woman sees
through glass streaking with bits
of clotted sky flown down.
Say the name of what watches her
from the window, now a watery mirror,

wavering. Tell her the face that's gazing
back at her—pale and round—
rose long ago, has since gone down.
Tell her about the moon
you've just undone.

Coat of Fur

Once she feels its weight
hang from her shoulders,
brushing the swing of her legs,
she forgets about clothes.
The coat is all she needs.

Lined with satin, cool and heavy,
darkest brown, this is skin
slipping loose from her wristbone,
smoothing her breasts.
Her body is free underneath.

The guard hair glistens
and follows her touch.
With a breath she can part it,
breathe it aside to find
the softness within.

Her nails quicken, curve,
her stride grows long. Somewhere
she catches the scent of moving water,
salt and spawn, and knows
she will never be cold again.

A Woman Remembers Water

When the sun and moon are painted
like changelings on her skin,
she moves downward.

She has no quarrel with stones.
Children of the rimrock,
they sing to her at night,

and a beaver's dam
is just a catch in her throat
as she falls down the canyon.

Rolling in her glacier bed,
she speaks to the wary trout
of salt and starfish and spume.

Touch her, follow her down.
An ocean is nothing to fear.
An ocean is only

darker sisters, darker bodies.

Where, Then Who You Are

In the mirror world beneath
my feet, there in the silver
world lying directly under.
There, that is where.

Rainbow who flows through
deepness, winnowed flesh
of pewter and rose. A window
into. That is who.

From out of sleep,
the liquid sigh who rises
to meet each footstep
I take, who makes a small

oval lake by rising
to fill each footprint
I leave behind.
Quicksilver water of where

I have been, path of mirror
to where I go, you are.
You, yes: river underground,
subterranean milk of stars.

In Her Palm, Perfection

Of course Persephone eats
some. Skin the red
of a heart's integument
streaked with gold.
Leathery. A faint wax
to her touch. Firm enough to be
an apple, but she knows it
won't contain a seamless meat.
Pomegranate—little
plummet of earthly heat.

How long could she have gone on
spying and plucking
meadow blooms, hand in hand
with her girlish chums?
How many bunches
of columbine, narcissus,
lily of the valley
before she would stray?

Red gives way
to pink underflesh.
That gives way to a membrane
of clotted white. Her long
half-moon fingernail
pulls this last skin aside,

prying the seeds
one by one from their bed.

True. This world could be bound
in perpetual winter.
Every month given away
to dark, to cold.
How *did* her tongue
stop at three seeds?

That's the trouble
with paradise. Things—
even jewels of such clear blood—
soon rankle.

Resolution

Arms, legs, and head gone,
only his marble torso still tenses
under her touch—she of whom remains
a single marble hand grasping his chest,
her thumb a little above
the hard bud of his nipple,
forefinger pressed to the hollow pulse
of his smooth underarm, the rest of her
broken away at the wrist

where her body parted from his.
They are the history
of strife. She an Amazon,
he a warrior, the two fused in battle.
Scars, those wounds fresh or imagined: so much
is erased from their ancient struggle,
so much from allegiances
they bodied forth
is now irrevocably gone.

The heat remaining is that enduring
heat of war—but broken,
crumbled, ground to a pale dust.
Shoulders and belly and groin,
he strains at her touch, yearns toward her
phantom body. Of this,

his enemy, only what merges
with his own flesh is left.
They are lovers, at last.

Pity

I know a woman who lives
inside the body of a bird.
I worry about her—
how she'll eat,
how she'll survive.
She's a spoonbill,
huge and pink and scarlet,
lovely except for her bill
flattened like someone
splayed it with a heavy boot.

I'm afraid people will laugh
at the way her wide gray mouth
hangs from the otherwise
perfect curve of her body,
at how she must sweep
those pie-plate lips
back and forth in the lake's muck.

What if someone says something
to hurt her? With great wings,
she lifts above me,
beating the air into submission,
trailing her long, jointed legs
as she goes. Not once looking back.

Work

This is the house
that must be entered,
the house whose doors
do not lock,
whose walls are shadow
of moving trees,

the house whose table
is heavy with food
already blessed,
waiting under
the mouths in need
of food, of blessing,

house whose windows
were polished until
they vanished,
whose moon and sun
once painted there
moved inside,

one whose chimney
breathes a visible
breath at night,
the house whose walls
must be swept
with the wing of a bird.

Making Do

All I do, I do with
fingers that carry
at each nail's quick

the first bit
of a moon rising
on the horizon.

All I do, I do
for the moon
lit like a candle

and set to float
down a wide,
winding stream.

Moon's light
turning every green
life to pewter.

Moon caught and wavered
along the surface
of a cup of watery

lies. Moon's boat,
moon tight in the
bowl of my eye.

The New Cosmology

So it's true: the poplar and I
are sisters, daughters of an ancient star,
every last thing

so much the same
(harp, toothpick, linnet, sleet)
that whatever I touch

is touching me, *whatever*
is a cousin
unremote. Even the metaphors—

ruby as blood, blood
as river, river as dream: all are true.
Just as the poets promised.

Psychopomp

Lay my body on this cool earth
a while. Rest me on my side.
Draw my knees to my breast,
curve the shadow of my fingers
over my eyes, let the shadow of ribs
shade the house where my heart
once lived. Under my cheek
place a small pillow of stone.

No bracelet to clasp the knob of my wrist.
No beaten silver to circle my neck.
If you care to give something precious,
leave a guide to show me the way.

Gather moon-white flowers,
spread them over my body.
Let petal, stem, and leaf
wither and drop to dust.
The shroud of sun that remains—
let only this pollen cover me.

Handwriting

—for Greg Simon

Vowels open their bodies—
cup, chalice, sloping bowl,
they spread out
in a string of sound.
From their depth
a breath,
breathing rises.

Each word takes its time
on the page, easing
from left to right—
each a source
of light, the line of ink
simply its shadow
left behind.

The connections are long
and curving. Dips
of a wren's near-
touches to the earth,
strokes of this skater's
journey across
a new moon of ice.

Translation

Empty of words, not empty
of light, the moon's face
awaits the touch of a pen.

Empty of ink, but not
of silver, that pale
slate that is the moon

waits for a sweep
of letters inscribed
in strokes deep as the dark

in which it floats.
Emptied of nothing, filled
with story, the moon becomes

a thin wafer melting
in the mouth, words
having found their tongue.

Who Shadows the Sun

—for F. G. L.

When the moon rises,
fields of bronze
bow down in gladness,
nighthawks spiral
up and up the cool
thickening air.

At the rise of the moon,
an egret hides its long
beak under a wing,
its white body a sister-
moon, low and pale.

Nothing must speak alone
in the light of a fullest moon.
Every voice is circled round
that high, silver song.

When the moon rises,
a sky parts to make room,
stars stand to one side,
the darkness both comes
and gives way.

The Same Worlds
Within You as Without

All bodies are the same,
concentric, all outside,
each inside what you

name as *self*—you, both
holder and held,
undistinguished from the chair

that cradles you,
from a cup suspended
in your hand, from the warm

infusion it contains.
Take a waxy leaf
from a magnolia and know

the leaf, the branch,
trunk and root have touched
you too. Have taken

your likeness inward.
That leaf's velvet underside is
your own downy

underbelly. One body,
and the one body's sole
instrument is itself. Lone voice,

singular song: moth-trill,
foothills solid with carol, a candle's
fattened croon of flame,

the warbling river
an endless stretched out body,
its breasts and bellies and thighs

turned skyward to sing—
dark and light, this one sun, moon,
one and everything.

When I Walk

I carry with me
salt in a small bag
muslin pouch
embroidered with a daylight moon
pale floss on pale cloth
an almost invisible crescent
to govern the fine shifting grains
of white sea held within

when I walk I carry
a bundle of straw
yellow stick white stick
palest of green stick
hard grasses that remember
a weight of seed curving them earthward
stiff grasses that recall
wind bending them down

walking   walking
I carry with me
a small stone smooth stone
blue veined stone
bottom of the well stone
weightless   ready for release
a stone that precise size and shape
to touch a body's vulnerable spot

as I walk I carry
three seeds of the red fruit
dropped from the red pod
three drops of blood
moments spent in the other world
bright seeds whose hulls
age to rust then brown then black
while in each seed
a pinprick of life
shines green   steady

when I walk I hold
a bone-handled knife
honed by those who sharpen
all that will take an edge
splinter knife   betrayal knife
father at the head of the table knife
ice I will melt in the sun knife

I walk and carry
a scrap of dark fur
my grandmother's winter coat
work of my grandfather's hands
the animal's lost voice
that glossy tongueless body

I walk with a handful
of my father's ashes
smoke in the air

word at the root of my tongue
small bits of bone drifting in gray
face of my face   ashes

walking I carry a name
written on a strip of bark
tree name   wisp of birchpaper name
slip of weeping yellow name
the name of skin that stretches and cracks
but does not break

I carry a hummingbird's nectar
my hands   enough
the honeybee's poison
my hands   light
a firstborn's silky caul
my hands   full

where and where I walk
and whenever I walk
I carry with me
these open hands

Appetite

Pale gold and crumbling with crust
mottled dark, almost bronze,
pieces of honeycomb lie on a plate.
Flecked with the pale paper
of hive, their hexagonal cells
leak into the deepening pool
of amber. On your lips,
against palate, tooth and tongue,
the viscous sugar squeezes
from its chambers, sears sweetness
into your throat until you chew
pulp and wax from a blue city
of bees. Between your teeth
is the blown flower and the flower's
seed. Passport pages stamped
and turning. Death's officious hum.
Both the candle and its anther
of flame. Your own yellow hunger.
Never say you can't take
this world into your mouth.

ACKNOWLEDGEMENTS

These poems, some in earlier versions, first appeared or are forthcoming in the following publications:

The Animal Bride (Trask House Press, 1994): "Manifesto," "Promise," "Cloth," "Oriental Lilies"

Calapooya: "Room," "Snow Red," "Where The Animal Goes When I Am Awake"

Clackamas Literary Review: "A Bride Of The World," " The Same Worlds Within You As Without"

Clearwater Journal: "Coat Of Fur"

CutBank: "Then She Is The Garden," "Pity"

Fabrication (26 Books, 1996): "Where, Then Who You Are," "Who Shadows The Sun," "Calling"

Fireweed: "Mirror Of These Eyes," "Small Acts of Devotion," "A Reading from the Erotic Compass of the World," "Making Do," "Words Rise from Nowhere Else"

Heliotrope: "Translation," "Speaking Of Dreams," "In Dreams"

Hubbub: "A Natural History," "A Little Primer on Sleep," "Graveyard Narcissus"

The New Republic: "Fabrication"

Pearl: "Calling," "The Day I Became A Woman"

O Poetry! O Poesia! Poems of Oregon and Peru (Oregon-Peru Poetry Project, 1997): "A Woman Remembers Water"

Poetry: "Haven," "Lullaby," "Resolution," "Handwriting," "When I Walk," "Appetite"

Poetry Northwest: "To Dream A Lover Away," "For The Love Of Sleep"

Seattle Review: "Second Skin"

Take Out: "What You Didn't Know About Money"

Talking River Review (Winter 2002): "Oriental Lilies"

Twelve Poets: "The New Cosmology"

Weber Studies: "Merman"

Wilderness Magazine: "Feral," "Work"

Willow Springs: "In Her Palm, Perfection"

Yellow Silk: "Not An Angel"

AUTHOR'S NOTE

PAULANN PETERSEN is the author of three poetry chapbooks, *Under the Sign of a Neon Wolf, The Animal Bride,* and *Fabrication.* A former public high school teacher in both Klamath Falls and West Linn, Oregon, she has taught poetry workshops for colleges and arts organizations, including Oregon Writers' Workshop and Creative Arts Community at Menucha. Her awards include a Wallace Stegner Fellowship in poetry at Stanford University and two Carolyn Kizer Poetry Awards. She lives in Portland, Oregon, where she serves on the board of trustees for *Friends of William Stafford,* organizing the January William Stafford birthday events.

COLOPHON

This book is set in 11 pt. Adobe Garamond, designed by Robert Slimbach based on the original classic designed by the sixteenth-century printer, publisher, and type designer Claude Garamond. The half-title is set in 20 pt. Adobe Garamond Semi-bold and the poem titles are set in 16 pt. Adobe Garamond Semi-bold italic. The cover title and section headings are set in Adobe Banshee, created by British type designer and lettering artist Tim Donaldson. This book was designed and produced by Robin Watkins using a Macintosh, Adobe software for publishing (Pagemaker, Photoshop and Acrobat) and Macromedia Freehand. The interior pages are printed on 60# Glatfelter Natural by Cushing-Malloy, Inc. A limited edition of 500 copies have been bound in boards, wrapped in dustjackets, and signed, numbered by Paulann Petersen.

308/500 *Paulann Petersen*